# FLORA AND FAUNA
# (HOMINIDS INCLUDED)

## ALSO BY ANTHONY HIRST

GOD AND THE POETIC EGO:
THE APPROPRIATION OF BIBLICAL AND LITURGICAL LANGUAGE
IN THE POETRY OF PALAMAS, SIKELIANOS AND ELYTIS
(Peter Lang, 2004)

MEMORIALS, NIGHTSCAPES, ETCETERA:
POEMS OF SEVERAL DECADES
(Colenso Books, 2020)


## AS EDITOR OR TRANSLATOR

ALEXANDRIA, REAL AND IMAGINED
edited by Anthony Hirst and Michael Silk (Ashgate, 2004)

C. P. CAVAFY: THE COLLECTED POEMS
Greek text edited by Anthony Hirst,
English translation by Evangelos Sachperoglou,
edited by Peter Mackridge (Oxford World's Classics, 2007)

THESE SCATTERED ISLES: ALONNISOS
AND THE LESSER NORTHERN SPORADES
by Kóstas Mavríkis, edited and translated from the Greek
by Anthony Hirst (Oxford Maritime Research, 2010)

THE IONIAN ISLANDS:
ASPECTS OF THEIR HISTORY AND CULTURE
edited by Anthony Hirst and Patrick Sammon
(Cambridge Scholars Publishing, 2014)

# FLORA AND FAUNA (HOMINIDS INCLUDED)

### NEW POEMS

### BY

### ANTHONY HIRST

DELOS PRESS

39 THE HURST  MOSELEY  BIRMINGHAM  B13 0DA  ENGLAND

First published 2021
by the Delos Press, Birmingham, England
delospeter@hotmail.com


ISBN 978-1-870380-42-3


Copyright © 2021 Anthony Hirst


The image on the front cover and all images in the text
are from photographs taken by the author.

# CONTENTS

*Time and place*     vii

## FLORA AND FAUNA

| | |
|---|---|
| Post-human world | 3 |
| Bees, birds and other bipeds | 4 |
| Bible — Babel — Fable — Augean Stable — What's on the table, Mabel? | 7 |
| Out of England | 10 |
| Food chain, Burgundy | 11 |
| Child management by phone, with rhyme | 11 |
| Greenhead Park, Huddersfield | 12 |
| Oh dear . . . | 14 |
| Gestation and digestion | 14 |
| On haiku and tanka | 15 |
| Welsh blarney in blank verse | 15 |
| Piscinery *or* Water tanka | 16 |
| Hibiscus night, Dragon-plant dawn | 17 |
| Generation or gender? | 20 |
| "Out of the strong came forth . . ." | 21 |
| Pigeon English | 22 |
| Piraeus | 23 |
| Detritus, trash, ordure, etc. | 24 |
| Requiescant in pace, but . . . | 26 |
| Seasonal variation | 26 |
| Talking of death | 27 |
| Voie unique | 28 |
| Response to a supposed response to the above | 29 |
| A family tragedy | 30 |
| A second death | 31 |
| And then a third | 32 |
| "blown . . . before the urban dawn wind unresisting" | 34 |

## CONTENTS

Rule Britannia with shield and fish spear — 35
A sentimental children's hymn revisited — 38
Crop rotation around Bossay — 40
A rude awakening — 40
"I could happily die here" — 41
Inconsequential Tuesday morning, late November — 44
Insecticide (a life of crime) — 45
Stages of oblivion — 50

## TREE-SPEAK

*Epigraft and Prolog* — 52
Dead tree rhyming haiku — 53
Mutilation — 54
A good marriage — 55
Bird on a branch — 56
Ozymandias — 58
Regimentation (pollards' reflections in 2020) — 60
Four musketeers — 61
Overcrowding — 62
Tree-house — 65
Isolation — 68
No success like failure? — 70
Regeneration — 71
Crucifixion — 72
Trees in Paradise — 73
Rites and wrongs — 76
Still from a horror movie — 78
Shame — 79
Trunk calls — 80
Robinson Crusoe or Moll Flanders? — 82
Words in lines — 84
Obscenity — 86
*Epilog* — 87

# TIME AND PLACE

All the poems in this book are published here for the first time, and practically all of them were written in the period from the spring of 2019 to the first months of 2021, and postdate almost everything in the much larger volume of my poems, *Memorials, nightscapes, etcetera: poems of several decades*, published in December 2020. Poems on pages 11 and 23 and a sequence of short poems on pages 24–25 belong to earlier periods, as noted in situ.

Many of the poems are explicitly connected with one or other of two places: the *Commune* of Bossay-sur-Claise in the southernmost part of the *Département* of Indres-et-Loire in Central France, where I have spent about a third of my time during the past five years, since, that is, my wife acquired an old farmhouse with a large garden there; and Stoke Newington in the London Borough of Hackney, where I have lived for most of the last forty years. Huddersfield, where I grew up and which I still visit every year or so, is the location of a single poem, though another, "Child management", was overheard on a TransPennine train approaching Huddersfield from Manchester, on the last stage of a journey from London to attend my cousin Chris's funeral, just days before the first UK lockdown came into force in March last year, and when social distancing was already in operation. "Greenhead Park, Huddersfield" belongs to the same day as the train journey. I walked through the park on my way up from Huddersfield station to the flat where I was going to stay — a flat belonging to an elderly relative, Jean, who was then in a care home and has since died. I don't think Chris, who was also my godson, ever had much truck with poetry (except for football chants). Nevertheless, I will dedicate this book, in which death — whether of flora, humans or other fauna — is a persistent theme, to their memory:

CHRISTOPHER GREENHALGH AND JEAN MARKS

*Anthony Hirst, Stoke Newington, March 2021*

# FLORA
## AND
# FAUNA

## POST-HUMAN WORLD

The Mind of Man —
Nature's failed experiment.
Best not repeat it.

The real Noah's Flood's
approaching now.
The work not of an angry God
but Noah himself.

"The animals go *out*
two by two" — species
driven to extinction.

Noah's Ark. Ark
of the Covenant.
But where's the Mercy Seat?
The Promised Land? It's all used up.

Shall we come to rest
on some Mount Ararat?
"No rest for the wicked."

The reckless child
has thrown out all its toys.
"The baby with the bathwater"?
Yes. Both have to go.

The earth's infected.
Stamp out *Homo virens*
and it might recover.

# BEES, BIRDS AND OTHER BIPEDS

Blackbird, female, in the road,
brown breast, down soft still,
flattened to left profile
by a passing truck.

Noise of water —
jet at centre
of a stone-lined garden pond,
a plastic heron standing by.

Delicious dirty honey smell —
a roadside stack
of cylinders of straw
greying in the sun.

The sheer quantity
of balls of mistletoe in trees
(especially poplars)
indicates perhaps

there's not much Christmas kissing here
and the UK's
late September spike in birthdays
is unknown.

Saint Martin's Way
old pilgrim route (now redefined)
from Poitiers to Tours
goes past our gate, then

enters woodland
where metal signs CHASSE INTERDITE —
raised white letters, background red —
are nailed to trees.

Now mostly painted out
(all white), holed by bullets,
twisted out of shape,
inverted, or torn down.

In a narrow clearing
by the rough green track
that cuts this patch of wood in two
a group of hives.

There the one sign in this woodland
that remains intact
and undefiled:
ATTENTION ABEILLES.

Bold are our defiant hunters
but their guns
afford them no protection
from the honey bee.

*continued over*

The Way turns right,
descends towards the river Claise
then left along the back road
winding into Bossay.

And on the grassy bank
beside that road I find
one of our more exotic birds:
a goldfinch.

Wings black, broad yellow band,
white spots; red patch around each eye.
Struck by a car.
Warm still in my hand.

CHASSE INTERDITE = HUNTING FORBIDDEN
ATTENTION ABEILLES = BEWARE BEES

## BIBLE — BABEL — FABLE
## — AUGEAN STABLE —
## WHAT'S ON THE TABLE, MABEL?

For a long time now we've been distinguished
from other mammalian bipeds
by wearing clothes, cooking and making tools
and also by our well-developed languages.

Then there's our eccentricity, exacerbated
in recent years by a growing tendency
to walk the streets — these too distinguish us —
talking to people who aren't there, or staring
fixedly into our little hand-held devices,
with which we fiddle constantly, occasionally
bumping into one another or a lamppost.

Consider too our less amusing quirks.
We are the earth's most self-divided species.
Male rivalry for dominance may be observed
in many species, rarely proving fatal.
Intra-species killing's a human speciality.
Murder is our trademark, the "mark of Cain":
gang and domestic murder, thoughtless youths with knives
and Second Amendment Americans with guns,
serial killers, deluded terrorists with bombs,
crimes of passion and murder in cold blood . . .
all orchestrated on a vast foul scale in WAR,
thanks to the insanity of powerful MEN.

Among the phrases that can stir male blood
are "total war", "weapons of mass destruction".
Let's not forget the electronic war games

that occupy so many minds from childhood on,
or that no other species is so bent — or bent at all —
on the destruction of its own environment.

No wonder it has come to this . . . Symbolically
in twenty-twenty, twenty-twenty-one —
numbers perhaps our most unfortunate
discovery — we must wear masks, for now
our very breath's acquired destructive power.

We like to think our well-developed brains
have brought us fine ideas, allowed us to create
things of great beauty and ingenious machines,
but our repressed self-knowledge always leaked
into our myths — of fratricide, of parricide,
of angry vengeful gods exulting in destruction.

In the Judaic myths there's a divine Creator, who,
seeing what He — of course it would be He —
had made, pronounced it good, though he had built in
the seeds of its destruction. And of course
it was a She who got the blame when Cain killed Abel,
setting in motion the descent to chaos,
prompting in time that petulant Creator
to become Destroyer, wipe clean the slate
and start again — with the same flawed ingredients,
for Noah's descendants are no different from Adam's.

And then the Christian absurdity
in which a god lets his own son be executed
in an ill-conceived attempt to "redeem" humanity,
whose faults "in the beginning" were his fault.

BIBLE — BABEL — FABLE — AUGEAN STABLE

But why expect a god to understand theology? —
that sublime feat of human idiocy,
converting fantasy into required belief.

And after that, one might conclude, this stupid god —
no better than the creatures made in his own image —
left it to them to wreak their own extinction
and maybe that of every living thing on this
his chosen planet that he's long grown tired of.

## OUT OF ENGLAND

This vast French garden — a farmer's field
just forty years ago, ploughed, as photos show,
right up to the back wall of what was then
an abandoned farmhouse — is indeed
    a *demi-paradise.*

Le bon Dieu has given us many trees
(none dangerous as far as we've been told)
and birds aplenty, but few animals.
No lions lying down with lambs.

The resident red squirrels are a great delight.
As are the hares that visit. Mice and rats of course.
And moles — those gifts of Satan — by the hundreds,
maybe thousands — all invisible
and working underground at night
to wreak their havoc in the greensward
    of this *other Eden.*

## FOOD CHAIN, BURGUNDY
### (JULY 2010)

En route, by bike. In the middle
of a narrow lane, a rabbit. Road kill?
Maybe. Stretched out, split open,
a crow pecking at its entrails.

In the moat at the Chateau de Sully
a bird, black plumage, spread-eagled
on the water, looks to be thrashing about.

Drowning? Trying to catch fish? No.
On closer inspection: Dead. The jerky movements?
A pack of frenzied fish tearing at its underside.


## CHILD MANAGEMENT BY PHONE, WITH RHYME
### (A MOTHER'S VOICE, VERBATIM)

Ah'll be 'ome soon.
So tell 'im to be'ave.
No. Put Jason *on*.

Jason, Ah'm ont' train from Marsden.
Ah'll be in Sla'waite in two minutes.
So Ah suggest
ya be'ave yaself. Right?
Else ya'll get shite.

## GREENHEAD PARK, HUDDERSFIELD

If you enter the Park by the bottom gates
(nearest to town) and set off up the wide avenue
before you, at twilight on a winter evening,
when the sun has only just slipped down behind
the rising ground ahead, take care not to miss
through fine fractal tracery of leafless trees
the harder thicker lines etched by the Chinese fretwork
of the bandstand roof — a sort of squat pagoda
floating in the air behind the knotted branches —
or closer, not far at all inside the gates —
and like the pagoda roof he's on the right —
the almost life-size bronze soldier from the Boer War
on his tall plinth with flowerbeds all around,
before you confront the famed memorial monument
to which this wide avenue is drawing you —
its fine broad flight of steps, stone-flagged terraces,
the urns and low stone balustrades (none of this
discernible now at this last breath of day),
the half-circle of the colonnade whose arms
reach out to embrace two wars' collective unnamed dead
(*that* you can see, black against the sky's receding gold)
and above it all the great stone cross. No matter what
you think of the origins of this grim symbol,
its crusading or triumphalist abuse,
you cannot fail to appreciate its force
standing at the juncture of the night with day, across
the moving frontier between the shrinking band of gold
and the slowly falling curtain of fast-darkening blue.

## OH DEAR . . .

"Distracted from distraction
by distraction",
I've left a long trail
of projects uncompleted.

Does time enough remain,
I wonder,
to put some of them to bed
before sleep overtakes me.


## GESTATION AND DIGESTION

Poem lies on the sheet,
man still sits up in bed, glad
to have got it out.

There's another one
scrabbling somewhere inside him
like indigestion.

Just a vague feeling
that seems to be reluctant
to get dressed in words.

Best leave it for now.
It'll soon be breakfast time.
It may need feeding.

## ON HAIKU AND TANKA

You've barely started
on seventeen syllables
before it's over.

But with thirty-one
even the most garrulous
may find space enough
to say something of import
before the final curtain.


## WELSH BLARNEY IN BLANK VERSE

"You're not the only person in the world
with high standards, refined taste . . . foresight . . . charm
and lovely hair" — words whispered in my eye
by a bag of *Real Sea Salt Crisps*, which has
been "packed in a protective atmosphere"
in Pen-Y-Fan Industrial Estate,
on Willow Road, in Crumlin, Newport, Gwent.
It's "Real Sea Salt", I am assured, and "not" —
how strange! — "the shoddy salt of donkey's tears".

# PISCINERY
### *OR*
# WATER TANKA

The lights for the pool
(switched on inadvertently
by a man who came
to change the filter) stayed on
all night — two groups of lanterns.

The night was windless,
the surface glass. Underneath
the pump made eddies
and on the bedroom ceiling
reflections softly trembled.

◆

In the dead centre
a single white feather floats
and underwater
a large bird flies upside down
high above dawn's sunlit clouds.

# HIBISCUS NIGHT, DRAGON-PLANT DAWN

Where, more than thirty years ago,
"the tall hibiscus [was] outlined
against faint streetlight filtered through the blind"
now stands the spike-leaved Dragon plant,

its seven winding woody stems
outlined against pale morning light
through curtains drawn so carelessly last night,
this cool spring dawn of early May.

Its stems have grown as though they had
encountered objects in the air
which they could only wind around
in their slow aspiration to the sky.

The pot sits on a folding stool — the pot
from which the Dragon grows, its rim
just level with the lowest point
at which the dawn light penetrates.

Thus the whole plant, above the soil,
is visible in silhouette
against disordered bands of different weave
which give the curtains their soft gauzy look.

Nourished haphazardly — some nights
a little, others none, some more —
with water in my bedside water glass
left over from the night before.

*continued over*

And still she "sleeps so easily"
(the hair long white that crowns her head).
"I sit up now beside [her] in the bed"
as on those nights so many years ago.

The plant has been replaced while we
have merely aged — now in the eighth decade
though not as yet too much the worse for wear,
we cultivate what lies to hand.

As for the poor Hibiscus, it has gone.
At first just relegated to
the back part of the sitting room,
where, out of direct sun, it ceased to bloom

and was eventually thrown out.
No more the "blood-red flow'r[s] of joy",
yet spiky leafsprays and those writhing stems
have their own pleasures for the eye.

Quotations in stanzas 1, 7 and 10, modified as indicated by square brackets, are from my poems "Saturday night and Sunday morning", "Night conceits", and "An Antique Valentine", on pages 56, 53 and 74 respectively of *Memorials, nightscapes, etcetera* (Colenso Books, 2020).

## HIBISCUS NIGHT, DRAGON-PLANT DAWN

*Stoke Newington, May 9th, 2020*

## GENERATION OR GENDER?

I listened to *The Moral Maze*
on Radio 4 the other night.
The topic: the divide between
the generations — had it been
exacerbated by the current
Covid-19 pandemic?
But much of the discussion turned
on large-scale politics.

I noted that only the women
among the panellists
and "expert witnesses"
talked of co-operation,
while on the whole the men believed
free-market competition
(left free of state restraint)
would sort the whole mess out . . .
eventually. One even blamed
the Welfare State for many
of our present ills.
It does seem clear
we can't be safe as long as most
of the decisions that affect our lives
are made by men (or would-be manly
types like Thatcher and Patel).

## "OUT OF THE STRONG CAME FORTH . . ."
### (JUDGES 14.14)

These martinets like Trump and Johnson,
Erdoğan, Putin, Bolsanaro, Xi and Kim,
who want to make their countries "great again",
when we have never needed their type less . . .

These primitives, these alpha males —
De Gaulle's supposed "La France c'est moi" the model
of their aspirations — these weak "strong men"
for whom their own, their country's "greatness"
means Domination; while "co-operation",
beyond lip service, is a dirty word —
unmanly, and beneath them . . .

The rich are rich by making others poor.
The strong are strong by making others weak.
The great are great by telling themselves so.

While their blood creed, their jungle law, has served
for other species to maintain the stock,
for *Homo sapiens* (self-styled, of course,
with unintended irony), whose *knowledge* turns
to power — the very opposite of *wisdom* —
it points to species suicide.

These "strong men" — mutant *Homo potens* —
don't heed warnings, but should surely know
that Hitler, Napoleon and Ozymandias
are types of their — and, with them, our — demise.

# PIGEON ENGLISH

Our garden is surrounded
by tall trees,
wood pigeons their largest
regular inhabitants.

Those birds' whole conversation
consists of one short sentence
traded back and forth
between the trees.

Bird talk is short on consonants
but the vowels
and placing of the emphases
are clear enough.

Mutual admiration
is, it seems, all
that these pompous loud-mouthed birds
are able to express.

But why birds resident in France
should speak in English
is something
I'm unable to explain.

I wish I'd never realized
just what it is
these boring birds
are saying to each other.

Once understood, though,
it's unforgettable
and I'm so tired now
of hearing all day long

in scarcely varied tones of voice
"You're so-o-o coo-oo-ool, bay-bee-ee-ee."
"You're so-o-o coo-oo-ool, bay-bee-ee-ee."
"You're so-o-o coo-oo-ool, bay-bee-ee-ee."


## PIRAEUS

(3 SEPTEMBER 2000)

Rusting freighters
lie idle in the sea lanes.
Inshore, small fish
forage among floating debris.

The water's
dimpled surface
fragments the ship's reflection,
pieces of the upper deck float free.

## DETRITUS, TRASH, ORDURE, ETC.
(VARIOUS DATES BETWEEN 1970 AND 2010)

### WINTER FOLIAGE

It's March at last and city trees
are coming slowly into leaf.
Eventually the spreading green
will help — to some extent — conceal
their winter foliage of plastic bags.

### CANALSIDE SIGHTS

There beneath the window
the canal's black glass reflects
an office building's
glittering façade.

And here a capsized shopping trolley
gives new meaning
to this disused
"commercial waterway".

And near the other bank
scarcely half-submerged
two armchairs sitting side by side
untenanted.

### OLDE-FASHIONED SEX IN SHOREDITCH

"Striptease" (in slender neon tubes)
with your pint
in "Ye Olde Axe"
(hand painted Gothic lettering).

LOVE IN THE GUTTER

An early-summer-morning walk.
The high street pavements cleansed by rain.
A used condom in the gutter — a knot
tied near the open end — tossed,
I imagine, from a passing car.

CUSHELLE

This toilet paper is embossed
with fluffy-eared koala bears.
While I can think of human faces
one might well want to smear with faeces
(some politicians and the super-rich),
surely no animal deserves
that particular abuse.

IN CORFU TOWN

The square is bounded by three churches,
a bank, two cafés and a bookshop.
The stone man on the pedestal
was once prime minister. A pigeon
is comfortably settled on his head.
His hair is slowly turning white.

## REQUIESCANT IN PACE, BUT . . .

In Bossay the recycling bins
for paper and for glass
are set close by the southeast corner
of the cemetery wall.

I'm happy to provide the dead
with varied reading matter
to help them wile away
their endless days.

I hate to think, though, of their peace
shattered repeatedly each day
by noise of breaking glass, going on
for minutes at a stretch.


## SEASONAL VARIATION

"If winter comes," as Shelley asks
the autumn wind, "can spring be far behind?"

Yet when spring comes, we're wont to say
that winter is behind us, summer still before.

## TALKING OF DEATH
"MISTAH KURTZ — HE DEAD"
(JOSEPH CONRAD, *HEART OF DARKNESS*)

I hate to hear that someone's *passed away*
and even more that some American
has *passed*. These euphemisms would, I think,
offend the dead — if they could take offence.

Grant them the stark simplicity of *died*
for that non-act with which each life must stop;
or, like the BBC reporting on
the day's or day before's events, *has died*.

(Today Sir Terence Conran's turn,
twelfth of September twenty-twenty.)

*Has died* — the present perfect — technically
is incorrect, and certainly should not
give way to the adjectival present, for the form
*is dead*, as we would rather not acknowledge,
can only be self-contradictory —
a verbal phrase for which no subject can be found.

# VOIE UNIQUE

"Voie unique" — an apt description
of life's journey, which is not
just "one way" from birth to death,
still less is it "single track"
for most of us, but "unique",
certainly, for each and every one:
the departure from a point
that none of us remembers,
the travelling some meandering road
that leads definitively nowhere
where everything will be forgotten.

Think, though, while you still can
of all you've seen, touched, tasted,
smelled, heard, imagined, felt
and realized along the way.

*A road sign and the narrow bridge across a railway cutting that it refers to*
*(Bossay-sur-Claise, June 16th, 2020)*

## RESPONSE TO A SUPPOSED RESPONSE TO THE ABOVE

Please don't tell me that I need the hope
that religious faith affords.
I'd be much less happy if I thought,
even for a moment, there was any
scrap of truth in all that Christian talk
of "the resurrection of the body
and the life everlasting"
to be spent in some imaginary
Paradise each person fashions
to conform to her or his desires,
where lions lie down with lambs
and Jehovah's Witnesses
check the number of arrivals —
there's an immigration quota, as you know:
just one hundred and forty-four thousand —
the measure of your elitist God's contempt
for the vast majority of humans —
and probably not a bunch of people
I'd want to live with for eternity.

## A FAMILY TRAGEDY

"There's a dead bird just outside the front door."
"Yes, I heard something bash against the glass
about an hour-and-a-half ago."

A female blackbird. The flies — greenbottles —
already on to her. And ants have done
some damage to her eyes. Her legs bent,
and her talons, rigid now.
                         Lunch is ready
so I can't bury her immediately
but put her in a plastic bag to keep the insects off.
Strange — given my intention to consign her
to the insects of the soil. But in darkness,
where her eyes would not have served her anyway.

A pair of blackbirds normally produce
three — and sometimes even four — broods per year,
with young still in the nest as late as August.
And it's only June.
                    Male blackbirds are among
the very few whose song's not predetermined.
They have the ability to improvise.
I wonder if tonight I shall detect
the tones of mourning of a newly single father.

She rests now, like some ancient much-mourned
Chinese maiden, under a weeping willow,
for grave cloths wrapped in maple leaves.

## A SECOND DEATH

A few days later.
Another female blackbird.
A different glazed door.
The same result.

Buried with less ceremony, perhaps,
than her sister, and not so deep,
between two layers of maple twigs,
with leaves too small for wrapping
but with wingèd seed pods
to speed her on her way.

Our very way of life — those large
glazed openings in our buildings —
presents a lethal threat to these poor birds.

A dead rat found in the front courtyard
I can treat as refuse, not these birds
whose partners' song is so enthralling,
who, of all birds, seem most like us —
hardly surprising, then, that we
can be the cause of their demise.

## AND THEN A THIRD

And then a third. Some three weeks later.
September first. Just after lunch
I go towards the living room
and at the door am startled by
a loud THWUMP as though someone had
flung something soft and heavy at
the patio door — and there, high up
on the glass I see a patch of what
looks like chalk-dust with wave-like patterns
suggesting an explosion.

Outside, two metres to the left,
almost two metres from the glass,
a large grey pigeon on its back.
It's still twitching, but, by the time
I get to it, it's altogether
motionless, its neck evidently
broken by the impact.

Looking more closely at the glass
I can see now the pigeon's ghost.
Its head can be made out. Its breast
is the explosion. Left and right
the lines of its spread wings.

I don't like pigeons,
don't like their noisy clumsy flight,
don't like their pompous strutting walk,
their stupid call, their petty squabbles
on the roof-ridge of the barn —
I've even thought I'd like to have

a gun to shoot them down.

But feeling implicated in
this fatal accident — this vast
expanse of glass the house's worst
death trap for birds and larger insects —
I feel that I must bury this poor pigeon.

A deeper grave than for the blackbirds.
Laid in a makeshift wooden coffin
(some strips of poplar bark pulled from
a rotting fallen branch nearby),
its head is folded down upon
its breast in the unnatural way
its broken neck allows.

I try to imagine that split-second's
shock in such a violent death before
the brain's switched off.

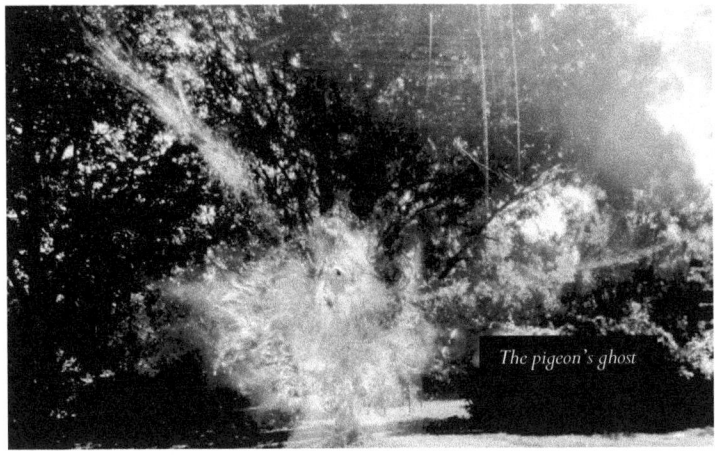

The pigeon's ghost

## "BLOWN . . . BEFORE THE URBAN DAWN WIND UNRESISTING"

(T. S. ELIOT, *FOUR QUARTETS*, "LITTLE GIDDING", II)

This wind has cleared the cobwebs from the sky,
the stars all polished to their brightest sheen.

It doesn't howl, it doesn't roar, but rumbles —
some vast machine approaching very slowly,
bent on the destruction of everything
that's in its path — and, getting closer, throws
up dust that threatens to obliterate
the stars far more effectively than dawn —
a dawn delayed — a dawn that may not come.

## RULE BRITANNIA
## WITH SHIELD AND FISH SPEAR
(AS SHE APPEARED ON OUR OLD PENNIES)

The early hours of the morning.
I'd been asleep for three,
have been awake for one.
It's now three twenty-five,
Sunday the thirteenth of December
in AD twenty-twenty.

Ursula von der Leyen
(iambic trimeter,
the ending feminine,
initial stress permitted
by rules of prosody)
will at some point today
deliver the decision
the European Union
has made about my country.

*My country right or wrong?*
My country wrong — so very wrong —
in its pursuit of "sovereignty" . . .

"absolute national sovereignty,
which," wrote Emery Reves
in nineteen forty-five
(*The Anatomy of Peace*,
published in June between
VE Day and VJ Day),
"causes anarchy
in international relations".

*continued over*

*Victory in Europe* once again
(and a trade deal with Japan!) —
is that what our PM is after?
Boris is indeed an anarchist
and we are living *in* —
may or may not live *through* —
a time when those least fit to rule
rise to the top, like bubbles from
putrescence in a stagnant pond.

This is the case, I think,
in several sovereign states
but not the European
Union, which, for all its faults,
for all of its mistakes,
alone among post-war
alliances and treaties
holds out to us a glimmer —
only a glimmer — of hope
for our benighted race.

◆

When the decision came,
quite early in the day
it wasn't a decision
but postponement, agreement
to resume the discussion
of a trade deal.

And two days on
while Ursula remains
cautiously optimistic,

Boris just keeps repeating
that the most likely outcome
is No Deal — a *fantastic*
outcome for Britain,
since from the First of January
we'll be able to do
*exactly what we want.*

This, one suspects, is what
*he*'s wanted all along:
to be the sovereign of a sovereign state,
a parlous, broken state
which he himself has wrecked —
swept to power on the crest
of a great wave of prejudice
and ignorance which he and Gove,
to keep up with Farage,
had fostered with their lies —
to be the architect of Brexit —
to "get it done".

And what a ghastly building
this hopeless amateur's designed,
this abject failure of a statesman.

RULE BRITANNNIA . . . RULES all the fish
beneath her WAVES, AND bankrupt BRITONS
NEVER    NEVER    NE-
                              VER
                                      SHALL
                                            BE
                                                  SLAVES.

# A SENTIMENTAL CHILDREN'S HYMN REVISITED

> All things vile and hideous,
> all misdeeds great and small,
> the mean and the invidious,
> a bored god's tried them all.

Each deadly fly that bites us
each buzzing wasp that stings,
he made their glowing colours,
he made their tiny wings.

*All things vile . . .*

The rich man in his castle,
the poor man at his gate,
he made one rogue, one victim
condemned to low estate.

*All things vile . . .*

The tall volcanic mountain,
the pyroplastic flow,
tornadoes and tsunamis,
he made each cause of woe.

*All things vile . . .*

He sends the drought in summer,
the blight to kill the grain,
starvation and diseases
so children die in pain.

*All things vile . . .*

The burnt trees in the greenwood,
the fields where soldiers lie,
the dead fish in the water,
the dark and threat'ning sky.

*All things vile . . .*

He gave us eyes to see them
and lips that we might tell
how dread is the almighty
whose touch turns earth to Hell.

*All things vile . . .*

## CROP ROTATION AROUND BOSSAY

I like the edges of these fields
where the harvesting is never quite complete
and shoots self-seeded from last season's crops
spring up among new alien growth.

The taller oat-stalks or the odd sunflower
amongst the wheat, barley in the flax.
Minorities on the edges of society,
their older ways of life still hanging on.


## A RUDE AWAKENING

You'd never have thought
that such a small red squirrel
could make that much noise
running over the roof tiles.

If it hadn't then
jumped down, appearing briefly
on the window cill,

I'd still have something
rather larger in my mind,
lying here, at dawn.

He may have died — the ageing man
whose shop this was — but whether "here"
or "happily" I've no idea.

Tyres, wheels, lights — spare parts for cars,

all second hand, and bric-a-brac (not much)
on shelves behind the glass — some vases,
some figurines in plaster, bronze,
ceramic, iron, the odd table lamp.
Such was his stock in trade.

There were two frogs in bronze I rather liked.
The price exorbitant — a hundred pounds.
I only wanted one but he
would only sell them as a pair.
Where are they now, I wonder.

When open — which was never every day —
there'd be some car parts set out on the pavement
or hung from the façade — two still remain
above the door, though why's not clear.

I noticed months ago the shop
was never open now. And then
one day a younger man — his son,
so I presumed — was clearing out
and left it almost empty — just two tyres,
two chairs, two shelving units, a step ladder,
a sink and piles of broken plasterboard
are all that can be seen inside.

He boarded up the door — the glass I think
was broken — wrote out on the board
his name and mobile number (which
I have redacted). And then that was that.

The bolder writing's come more recently.
The graphic signature looks like a dog —

four legs, raised tail, two pointed ears,
a strong suggestion that the dog is farting,
the face obscured by the attempt — half hearted,
to say the least — to spray it all out white.

Only a dog might die here happily
and even that I doubt.
Reflected in the window, though,
the vision of . . . "the other side".
Could that be Jacob's ladder on the right,
and heaven not too far above?

*Allen Road, London N16, March 4th, 2021*

## INCONSEQUENTIAL TUESDAY MORNING, LATE NOVEMBER

*The Observer*'s killer sudoku
bothering me for two days now
completed at the fifth attempt,
    in bed at six a.m.

Reversing the fifth A4 printout,
I face a blank page on my clipboard,
pencil in hand, but no words come
    more interesting than these.

Between the first and second stanzas
there was in fact a half-hour gap
in which, light out, I tried and failed
    to get to sleep again.

Then something scratching at the door
— my mind a dim-lit cluttered room.
I doze a while and in it comes:
    a word, a name: *Myrine*.

Greek. Three syllables: *Mur-inn-ay*.
And yet no woman of that name
in the annals of mythology
    seems relevant at all.

Perhaps I got it wrong, misheard,
misread, and it was simply *murine*.
Two syllables. Its meaning: "mouselike".
At any rate that would explain
    the scratching at the door.

## INSECTICIDE
## (A LIFE OF CRIME)

"As flies to wanton boys are we to th' gods;
They kill us for their sport", as Gloucester says,
viciously blinded in *King Lear*.

There's what I think of as a Buddhist streak in me
which cautions against causing harm
to any living thing. I make exceptions though;
and interspecies conflict, predation
and the food chain are part of natural disorder.

Highly reactive to the bites
of horseflies and mosquitoes, those I kill
whenever they come near me; hornets when,
sometimes at night, they get inside the house;
bluebottles whose insistent buzz
makes it impossible to concentrate;
ants by the dozen on the kitchen worktops.

When the infestation's serious I trace their routes
back to the point of entry, spend half an hour,
or more if needed, squashing every ant
that tries to cross the threshold either way,
to stem the flow of information —
feeler to feeler — that sustains their two-way traffic.

Twice in my life, though, I've engaged
in killing sprees which in no way at all
could have been said to serve my own self-interest.
Most recently — some twenty years ago,
that is to say — out walking on Hymettus,

## INSECTICIDE (A LIFE OF CRIME)

when living briefly on that side of Athens,
I sat down on a rock beside an ants' nest —
quite large the ants, more than a centimetre long —
and picking up a stick began to kill
the ants emerging from the nest,
becoming fascinated by the way
the living gathered up the dead
and took them back inside — for food?

The earlier mass murder pains me more
to recollect, though at the time
I can have been no more than ten years old.
A guesthouse in the Yorkshire Dales
to which my family with my cousins' family
in summer often went to stay,
we children sleeping in a hikers' dormitory.

Once on a walk with older cousin James
we came across a skull — ram's skull with horns.
Next day, taking my little haversack,
I climbed back up the fell alone, afraid,
and brought it back and put it on the shelf
above the fireplace of the room we slept in.
But then I didn't dare to go in there by myself,
the skull become a ghost that haunted me.
I don't know now the sequence of events,
and so, with muddled hindsight, I suppose
that that pale death's-head of an animal
accused me of the other deaths I'd caused.

It was in that same guesthouse that I wrote,
on lined blue letter paper with a pen,
at a small desk in a window recess my first —

or was it second — poem. (In memory it jostles
for priority with one about my dog.)
It was a sunlit afternoon
and I was looking through the window
into the spacious garden between house and road.
"As I sit here and gaze at the trees" —
so it began, and happily the rest's forgotten
except that the next line rhymed "bees" with "trees".
It may have been "the hum of bees"; and "birds"
were there as well — all part of an idyllic scene
conjured to fit some strange idea of what
adult poetry was like. I only hope
that holiday was not the same one
in which I massacred the bees.

I had a tennis racket and a ball
and I was playing somehow on my own,
and on the lawn, but down towards the gate,
and noticed not far off a stream of bees
flying upwards from the grass,
emerging from a hole — their nest beneath the ground.
I stood there with the racket, struck them one by one
as they came out and killed . . . a hundred at a guess.
There was an element of daring — and of danger:
they might have stung me, but none did.
I don't think anyone was watching me.
An adult surely would have intervened
if only to protect me from the bees;
one of my cousins would have joined me.
But no, I was alone, a wanton boy,
and killed them for my sport.

Some Saturdays and in the holidays

my school friend Howard (junior school, that is to say)
and I would play around the mill dam
(the woollen mill where Howard's father worked)
and fish for sticklebacks and minnows with our nets.
Sometimes we'd take them home in jam jars
and they'd soon die — not though what we'd intended.

Aged twelve, I think, I first tried fishing with a line.
On holiday again, this time the Isle of Aran.
Alone again, on a damp grey afternoon,
and from the pier I caught a fish.
Not big, about an adult handspan long,
and black. And, cold and slippery,
it wriggled in my hand, and now I did
just what I thought I had to do: pulled out the hook,
but roughly and there was a lot of blood,
then dashed its head against the boarding of the pier.
I was disgusted with myself. I felt unclean.
I threw the dead fish back into the sea
and I have never fished again.

Then, in my forties, walking in the hills of Crete
along a dirt road through a straggling village.
A woman in her narrow roadside garden
distraught, almost hysterical,
attacking with her broom a huge brown toad —
the largest toad I'd ever seen —
and crying "Poison! . . . Poison!"
she pushed it through the gate
and swept it — injured now — across the road
and stood there cursing still the broken twitching thing.
To put both toad and woman out of their distress
I took a rock and with both hands

## INSECTICIDE (A LIFE OF CRIME)

brought it down hard and squashed the toad.

From insects, fish, amphibian, moving up
the scale to mammals, leaving out the quadrupeds,
the crime that haunts me most, and to this day,
though it must have been the nineteen-seventies,
was one I didn't actually commit
since at the time I was asleep in bed.

I had a workshop in those days
where I made furniture to order.
There was an old man there. I don't know why.
A vagrant, although "tramp" 's the word attached to him.
I don't know what he said, but he was hassling me.
Annoyance mounted until something snapped
and in a fit of rage I killed him.
Maybe I strangled him, or smashed his head in with
a baulk of timber, or stabbed him with a screwdriver,
or with a chisel; but that part of it is lost.

In front of the workshop, a small secluded yard
and there, an open excavation
as though I had been working on the drains.
That's where I buried him, and though it didn't happen
the guilt, the secret knowledge of my crime
still weighs on me each time it reappears
even though nearly fifty years have passed.

But time is not a measure known to dreams.

## STAGES OF OBLIVION
## (A DEFECTIVE SONNET)

There is dementia to look forward to.
Bits of your brain will start to fall apart
and you will lose whatever sense of self
you may have had, and fail to recognize
the people from the life that you're forgetting,
or drift off into earlier stages of that life.

At first, maybe, acute anxiety
while you still sense that there are things you've lost.
With luck this will give way to equilibrium.

One consolation (though you won't perceive it such) —
you may forget that one day you must die
and when death comes you won't know what it is.

[The last two lines are missing.]

# TREE-SPEAK

# EPIGRAFT AND PROLOG

*And [Jesus] cometh to Bethsaida;*
*and they bring a blind man unto him,*
*and he led him out of the town;*
*and when he had spit on his eyes,*
*and put his hands upon him,*
*he asked him if he saw ought.*
*And he looked up and said,*
*I see men as trees walking.*
                    (MARK 8.22–24)

But I with my
      peculiar brand
of distorted
      sight and hearing
see and hear
      trees as men talking —
not only men
      but women too.

# DEAD TREE RHYMING HAIKU

Near Much Hadham, Hertfordshire, May 20th, 2020

Dead though I may be
what else is there here to see
livelier than me?

# MUTILATION

I used to think
    I was a tree
but after all
    you've done to me
I'm not so sure.

But when I wear
    my summer dress
I can at least fool
    most of you
and feel more easy
    in myself.

*Clissold Park
from Stoke Newington Church Street,
London N16, February and June 2020*

# A GOOD MARRIAGE

Side by side we've stood and grown
through several of your generations.
The space between our trunks we share,
each extending limbs beyond the unseen
centre line, for the most part lightly entwined,
here and there, though, tightly clasped.
But I on my west side, he on his east —
there we can grow without conscious restraint,
yet form harmonious asymmetry.

*La Gilletterie, Bossay-sur-Claise, on the road to Tournon,
looking southeast, June 27th, 2020.*

## BIRD ON A BRANCH

We know we're just dead branches
from several different trees
waiting to be cut up and burned
to keep you warm in winter.

But for this bird we constitute a tree.

He's picked our topmost branch
as vantage point from which, secure,
he can assess the threat you pose
with your unlawful entries to the barn
where his and one more family
have made their modest summer homes.

*La Gouarie, Bossay-sur-Claise*
*July 13th, 2020*

# OZYMANDIAS

*My name is Ozymandias*, once *king of* trees,
the tallest of some sixty in my small domain.
Unlike my namesake in *an antique land*,
I need no other poet to scoff at my demise.

Illusions of grandeur were never my undoing.
It was my height and my position at the corner
of this plot, for I was struck repeatedly
by lightning during three successive years
of winter storms. The first two years I carried on;
my fallen limbs lay round me. In the third
I lost my last main living limb, and could produce
so little leafage on my few more recent shoots
that I then starved to death, unable to sustain
even the shelf-fungi protruding from my sides —
my veins ran dry, and they turned black and died,
but cling on, hard as stone, bonded to my bark,
which will be shed, a little at a time, before
I crumble to a formless heap of rotting wood.

Still, though, I *stand*, a crownless, limbless, broken trunk,
while *round* this garden with its sixty living trees
the undulating farmers' fields *stretch far away*.

*La Gouarie, Bossay-sur-Claise*
*July 19th, 2020*

# REGIMENTATION
## (POLLARDS' REFLECTIONS IN 2020)

Not only were we badly mutilated
in our youth, or remodelled, if you like,
to suit these bipeds' views of what
trees should be like and how they should behave,
but also, earlier, were planted
in this unnatural and rigid grid,
spaced out so uniformly from each other.

*Preuilly-sur-Claise, July 24th, 2020*

Recently we've been able to derive
some satisfaction in observing
that bipeds have been forced, like us —
although, it seems, by things too small
for their control — to practice social distancing.

## FOUR MUSKETEERS

They planted us to be a hedge.
We stood our ground and here we are
four stalwart trees who serve
   no human purpose.

Marchebec, Bossay-sur-Claise, looking southeast, September 10th, 2020

## OVERCROWDING

When we were young — the hornbeams and the oak
on my north side and I, an ash,
set in our places by a female human
and her father some forty years ago —
there was sufficient room for all of us.

But as we grew, each faring better
on the southern side, it became quite clear —
and clearer year by year — that we'd been planted
far too close to allow our full maturity.

A well-made garden should not be a battleground,
a site for rivalry, the struggle for existence
of a natural forest, but a place of privilege
where each tree may attain with dignity
its proper form and stature.

The hornbeams and the oak, reaching for the sun,
encroached upon my northern side.
The hornbeams to my west as well as north,
the oak just slightly to my east, extended
branches which shaded from the evening
and the morning sun my northern side
where my own branches ceased producing leaves,
then died, dried out, some rotted and broke off.

The new custodians of this garden helped
a year or two ago by cutting off —
for their own purposes no doubt —
some of the hornbeams' branches closest
to their house, but it was, I think,

too late for me. (Five hornbems there were once but two are now just ivy-shrouded stumps — again the work of the custodians.)

La Gouarie, Bossay-sur-Claise, looking east, August 8th, 2020.
The ash on the right, the oak on the left, between and behind them
the walnut tree, some hornbeam branches in the left foreground.

The modest walnut, between the oak and me

but to our east, has suffered less from overcrowding.
Its branches not so sturdy as they might have been.
Its shape, though, much more regular than ours.

Red squirrels chase each other through our branches
and leap from tree to tree. Their antics
afford us some amusement. But the pigeons
are just annoying with their clumsy flight.
Their noisy wings disturb our foliage each time
they launch their fat grey bodies from our limbs.

And I, I'll carry on for years or decades yet —
who knows? — disheartened by the certainty
my blighted northern side will not regrow.

# TREE-HOUSE

At first you thought I was a bush or clump of trees.
Now don't deny it. But then you were puzzled
by my shape — my four straight sides
    and all that curly hair on top.

*On the east side of the old railway line, between
La Chainaye and La Gilletterie, Bossay-sur-Claise,
September 12th, 2020, looking southeast.*

I am of course a small two-storey house
(one room, a loft, a ladder once between),
as you soon realized when you came round
    to my south side and saw

# TREE-HOUSE

the patch of roof tiles showing through the leaves
and that dark space at bottom centre —
which is of course a doorway.

*Looking north*

Yes, yes, please enter (mind your head)
and see the fireplace and a pile of logs
that no one now will ever use.
Why light a fire when my door has gone?

One of the many small field houses
that you have wondered at in farmland here,
left from another era — and I . . .
am by no means the smallest, I would add.

# ISOLATION

Alone here in the middle of this field,
my solitary life at least *is* life.

I am an inconvenience to those
poor bipeds who work the soil from their machines
and yet they've watched me grow and never cut me down.
Must I, then, have some weird significance for them?

My field is bounded on three sides by narrow roads
and on the fourth, the east, a disused railway line,
marked now by a double line of trees — my nearest kin,
with those on the north side where the road is steepest,
its lower stretch divided from the field
by a narrow strip of woodland and some gardens
with trees along their boundaries here and there . . .

Too far away for any news to reach me.
No decent rain for months, the summer ends,
the bipeds all uneasy, and I? —
I wonder what the future holds.

*Looking southwest, August 31st, 2020*

*Looking northwest from the Lureuil road towards the first house in La Chainaye*

The field is adjacent to the hamlets of La Gouarie and La Chainaye in the Commune of Bosssay-sur-Claise.

Looking northeast. Background, from left to right: the "narrow strip of woodland", the garden trees of La Gouarie, the "railway line, marked now by a double row of trees".

## NO SUCCESS LIKE FAILURE?

Yes, I admit it.
Masquerading as a tree
and — to make it worse —
opting for a concrete trunk
really wasn't very bright.

But I tried. And failed —
with results that you can see —
though not entirely . . .

for now my bleached bones
match the concrete perfectly
and as a dead tree
I'm rather more convincing
than I ever was alive.

*Les Rocheraux,
Bossay-sur-Claise
September 18th,
2020*

# REGENERATION

*Petit Saint Lifard,
Bossay-sur-Claise,
September 22nd,
2020*

From the broad grey trunk
cut through years past by lightning
grew I — a new trunk,
narrower, but just as tall —
true offspring of my own corpse.

# CRUCIFIXION

*My* crucifixion —
I am both cross and body
but not less the pain.

The crowd as ever
in attendance but my fate
isn't their concern.

# TREES IN PARADISE

Here we three stand among lamp-posts and cars,
in between Shelley House and Binyon House
with Blake House there behind us in the background.
Milton Gardens Estate — so many poets
memorialised in post-war public housing.

Whether these Gardens be *Paradise Lost*,
or *Paradise Regained*, you must decide —
a matter not of our, but your estate.

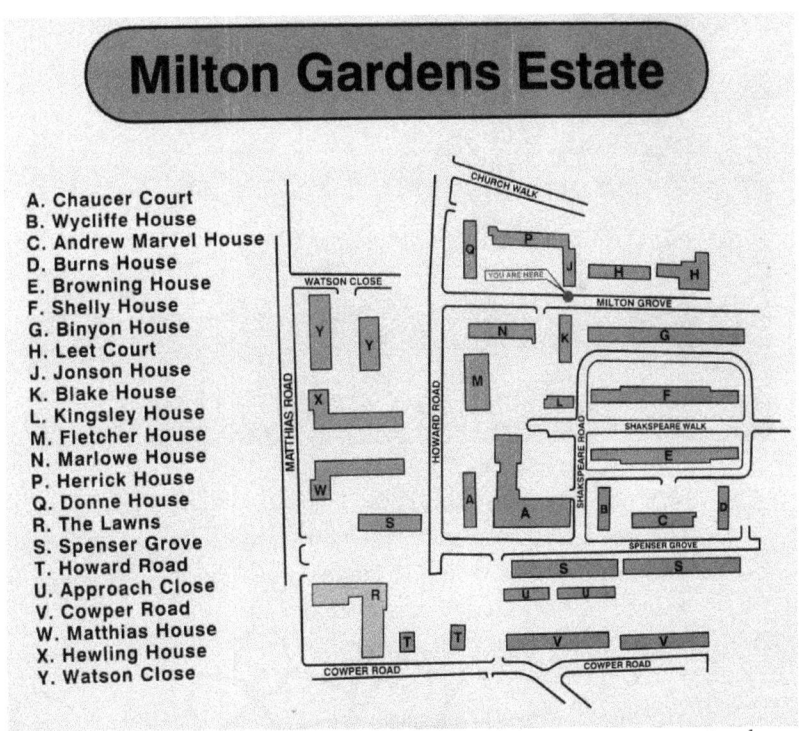

*continued over*

*Blake House and Binyon House, London N16, November 30th, 2020*

We don't suppose this is the Garden which
the Lord God planted to the east of Eden
and none of us is going to claim to be
a Tree of Knowledge or a Tree of Life —
we're just a group of urban refugees . . .

Street trees, street people — but it's us who are

better adapted to sustain that role.
Homeless, but then we have no need of home.
We shall not die of hypothermia.
For us the threat's municipal attention,
which my companions have already suffered.

I, the youngest and shortest of the three,
almost unharmed and in my natural state,
still perhaps — you judge — "pleasant to the sight",
will stand for Shelley since his life was shorter,
so much shorter than those of fellow poets
in our immediate vicinity,
though death by drowning's not what I expect.

My lofty bifurcated neighbour, sprouting
from those unnatural knots above
and having very little lower down
must play the part of Laurence Binyon.
Distorted by his background and
his education, little of what he wrote
rings true; he voices public sentiment
and rarely is it possible to sense
a living breathing man behind the words;
he has grown old and age has wearied him.

Behind us and the closest to Blake House,
our friend has triumphed over mutilation
and has achieved a truly joyful
wildness of form, worthy of Blake's
contorted fantasies in lines both drawn and written.

Three of the many poets in Milton's Paradise.

## RITES AND WRONGS

The birthday of some obscure preacher
some twenty centuries ago
and in the "bleak midwinter". . . Bleak
indeed for turkeys and for us
young conifers, both sacrificed in millions
to appease or please, we must suppose,
some ancient god who still revolves
in the outdated brains of humans,
the planet's most destructive creatures
and, sadly, its most powerful —
a second Age of Dinosaurs.

The turkeys slaughtered, feathers all
pulled out, their heads, necks, feet cut off
before they're roasted in the ovens —
a holocaust, the *almost whole-burnt* offerings.

Our trunks sawn through not far above
the ground, we leave our roots behind
but do not die immediately.
The bipeds need us to survive
two weeks or more, festooned with baubles,
little figurines and "fairy" lights
inside their overheated homes,
without too many of our needles
falling off and messing up their carpets —
two weeks from just before that birthday
to twelve days after, when we're stripped,
tossed out into the streets and left
for bin-men to collect for composting —
better at least than being mixed

with all the rest of human junk,
dumped and compressed in landfill sites,
some bipeds having grasped at last
(and probably too late for all
of us) recycling is the way
that nature, before their more recent drastic
interventions, sustained herself, and us.

*Milton Grove
London N16
January 8th, 2021*

# STILL
# FROM A HORROR MOVIE

If the expression
"writhing in agony"
should come to mind,
you'll have some idea
of what it feels like
to be such as I am,
and were my state
natural, the phrase
"malignant Creator"
might reach your lips.
But no,
I was well made
and flourished once
till much of me
fell victim
to some deranged
chainsaw-wielding
so-called
Tree Surgeon
and I must now
embody
an aberration
from a biped's brain,
or have become,
if you prefer,
a Work of Art.

*Clissold Park, London N16, January 25th, 2021*

# SHAME

Yes, I and my immediate companions,
grown tall, put this west-facing housing row,
through no fault of our own — we were here first,
in shadow and the powers-that-be declared
    we must be dealt with.

Some of my companions reduced to stumps —
a fate perhaps more dignified than mine
(except this giant hedgehog next to me).
No wonder that my few remaining branches
grow downwards — not only to avoid the height
for which we were condemned — not just from fear,
for, were I made like bipeds in their houses,
    I'd hang my head in shame.

Clissold Park
and Queen Elizabeth Walk,
London N16, January 17th, 2021

# TRUNK CALLS

Clissold Park and Green Lanes,
London N16, January 25th, 2021

*Our* crime was not that we put anyone in shade.
As we grew tall and stretched our west-side branches out
beyond the railings of the park, over the pavement
and then the roadway of Green Lanes, we used to find it
irritating, the way in which the big red buses
clipped our wings (as our good friends the birds might say).

Green Lanes — an ancient name attesting to our forbears'
presence — the Motor Age has made a major route —
an A-Road at any rate, the A-One-O-Five —
escape route from the horrors of the capital
we'd be inclined to say — stretching eight miles from here
to Enfield Town (handy for the M-Twenty-Five and the
A-Ten), making it one of London's longest streets.
But buses, it's now clear, count for far more than trees.

Repeated trimming proved too tiresome and expensive.
More drastic measures have reduced us to the state
you now observe. We are just posts, sprouting at most
a few twigs from our wounds — last flickerings of life.
With insufficient leafage to sustain us, sooner
or later, we'll give in, resign ourselves, and rot.

## ROBINSON CRUSOE OR MOLL FLANDERS?

I am what you lot call a *eucalyptus* tree.
"Well covered", I'm afraid, is all that fine word means,
referring only to one minor feature
of our anatomy which caught the attention
of one of your great botanists — that is,
to the *operculum*, a woody cap
which covers each one of our spiky flowers
as they develop. But I'd like to think that it
might also mean "well covering", for I have heard
in India and Sri Lanka we've been used
for shade and windbreaks in the tea plantations,
and I suspect that's where I'd rather be
though in my crippled state I'd be no use for that.

Instead, I find *myself* in shade and never glimpse
the sun at all in winter months, stuck here
behind the north façade of this grand building,
in former times an educational establishment,
the Daniel Defoe School — he lived nearby —
and then a Further Education College,
converted now to luxury apartments,
renamed, ironically, Scholars Place.

Look at my wretched state. I am a joke,
a travesty of what a tall, upstanding and
fast-growing eucalyptus tree should be.
Some accident or act of vandalism
when I was very young (I don't remember)
or was it a genetic defect (I don't know)
condemned me to this stunted and distorted growth.
It's strange that I was not ripped out, replaced

by some more healthy specimen, and I suppose
I am indebted to municipal neglect
for my survival, my unhappy life,
but I'm not sure I'm grateful to your kind for that.

Ayrsome Road, London N16, January 21st, 2021

    Oh what a tale of woe
    your Mister Defoe
    might have devised for me!

# WORDS IN LINES

I was an evergreen, a conifer,
in some unnatural commercial wood
(we grew in neat rows there, well-spaced, it's true)
in far-off Scandinavia.

*January 8th, 2021*

Selected for the straightness of my trunk,
cut down, my tapering upper part cut off,
stripped of my branches and my bark
and fed through a machine which trimmed me up
and made me what you see today — a pole,
perfectly circular in my cross-section,
and my diameter unvarying
from "head to toe" as bipeds say.

I might, if I had been less tall, less straight,
have led a very different afterlife,
as many of my old companions did,
been cut up small and pulped for making paper
and ended up as newsprint or the pages
of books and magazines, letters, reports,
bus tickets, till receipts, prescription forms . . .
My kind, you see, are everywhere,
dispensing information among bipeds.

Of course, *I'm* in communications too,
distributing the phone lines to some houses —
the older ones, that is — in Albion Grove
(the modern ones have underground connections)
in Hackney, London N16, UK.

All in our different ways transmitting words
between those little creatures who have come
to dominate and desecrate the earth.

Bipeds need languages because they've lost
all direct access to each other's minds
and live as separate individuals,
antagonistic, practically devoid
of any common purpose. Not perhaps
the pinnacle, as some of them suppose,
of evolution's gradual ascent.

Random mutation, natural selection,
don't forget. Survival of the fittest —
but are you *really* sure that's you
or that you really *will* survive?

# OBSCENITY

*Aden Terrace, London N16*
*3 March 2021*

I am the extent
of the obscenity
of what you humans
do to us

when our height
or density
gets in the way
of your designs.

Kinder surely
to have cut me down
than hacked me about

and left me here
in such a hideous
and pitiable state.

## EPILOG

Already, in late February,
the world is turning green again
but I'm not sure I've had my fill
    of winter trees,

their form far more expressive now,
more individual, than in
their foliage. Take those of just
    a single species . . .

Each has its distinct character,
the number and the pattern of
its branches its and its alone —
    no two alike —

telling the story of its growth,
its struggles, bursts of energy,
natural accidents, and acts
    of vandalism.

Each is its own history
in living form, unfathomably
rich in detail, more eloquent
    than our anatomies,

tense and majestic in the stillness,
wild in the howling wind, at play
and dancing in the gentle breeze,
    while in the dark

it may seem cruel and ominous,
clutching the moon among its tendrils;
far more resilient than we
    can ever be.

But do trees envy our mobility?
Or see it as poor compensation
for our detachment from the earth,
    our rootlessness?

See how disdainfully they all
look down on us. We are, at worst,
an irritant, or so some think,
    not knowing we

poor bipeds may have planted them
and without warning there may come
a day when we for our own ends
    will cut them down.

Lightning Source UK Ltd.
Milton Keynes UK
UKHW021525210821
389240UK00009B/137